MW00787801

NURTURING

Quotes to Inspire You Toward Better Relationships

NOTES

VINCE SHIFFLETT

ISBN: 978-1-73597-572-6
ISBN: 978-1-73597-573-3

TABLE OF CONTENTS

INTRODUCTION

Have you ever paused just to think about your relationships? This could include your romantic partner, friends, and family. Would you consider them healthy relationships that contribute to your life in a positive way? Do they help you grow as a person? Do they fulfill you?

If you've never given much thought to the people you invite into your life, then you've come to the right place to help you take a closer look at your relationships. Why is this important? Because adjusting can lead to healthier, happier, and longer lasting ones. All our relationships work synergistically with one another. In other words, if our relationship with self is not good, then it will impact all our other relationships. If the relationship with our mind is a troubled one, then again, our other relationships will most likely be off balance.

In the upcoming chapters, I share quotes along with my corresponding thoughts that are sure to create change and stimulate self-healing in all your relationships. Whether you seek a healthier relationship with self, your mind, your spirit, or your significant other, all you need to cultivate a balanced life is at your fingertips. This book will change the trajectory of your relationships and lead to greater peace and happiness.

May this book inspire and encourage you!

Phase One: Nurturing Notes for Better Relationship with Self

"Want a happier life? Learn to detach."

When you are bound to the past, you are not free to grow. You must detach from anything that holds you back to be open to opportunities for growth. Attachment to the wrong things impairs growth. Are you ready to nurture the new?

Attachment can lead to suffering. It is only when we realize that nothing lasts forever that we are more equipped to deal with loss. Loss is inevitable. Nothing lasts forever, not even our own lives. Live in the present and hold people you love with a loose grip.

I have come to realize that there is a beginning, middle, and end to everything. The ending can be painful, but it can lead to personal growth to the degree that we are willing to accept the ending and learn from the experience.

A good example of this was when I was riding our public transit train the other day, I became aware of how the train would make many stops before reaching my destination. At each stop, people would get off and new people would get on. No one stays on the train forever. When your stop comes, you are getting off. Again, it can be painful when your stop comes, or it is time for someone you love to get off the train. The beauty in it all is that someone new is getting on the train. If we are unable to detach and allow the old to get off and the new to get on, it can lead to emotional upheaval and negatively impact the relationship we have with ourselves.

Detach from the old and begin to nurture the new.

"Stand in the beauty of your Authentic Self."

For much of my life, I tried to be what others had taught me I should be. I tried to live the life that had been deeply indoctrinated in me as the "right way" and the "only way," as opposed to living my authentic life. I didn't know how to live as the beautiful, unique expression of the divine that I was created to be. I have grown to realize that your "right way" and my "right way" may be totally different. And that's okay. As the ole saying goes, "just because someone is on a different path than you does not mean they are lost."

Authenticity is another name for freedom. Freedom to be yourself. When you let go or detach, the smokey layers of life may disappear. The clouds yield to the bright light of the true you. Fear not—you will be with *you*. There's no one better to be with than yourself! Be sure you enjoy being with you.

Be yourself. No one else can be you.

"Taking a pause when you need a
pause is a gift to yourself."

In the busyness of life, sometimes we forget to breathe. We forget to sit in the moment. Taking a pause brings you into the now. The pause helps you detach and places you in your best space. Your truth lies in the peace of the pause.

Taking time out for self is essential. It sends a message to your brain that you are worthy. That you are human. That you are more than your to-do list. It can be easy to get all caught up with work and life in general and not remember to take the pause when you need it. Take time to nurture self for greater self-growth and a healthier relationship with self. Remember, your relationship with self is foundational to all other relationships in your life.

"Want a healthier relationship with others?
Cultivate a healthy relationship with self-first."

A healthy relationship with self involves nurturing the spiritual, mental, and physical aspects of our being. We must carve out time to spend in each area daily. The way you do this is unique to each person. A balance of a healthy body and healthy mind help to create the sacred space needed to connect with spirit and cultivate that relationship with self.

If just one wheel on your car is out of balance, the car will not run smoothly. It is the same for your being. If the spiritual, mental, or physical part of your being is out of balance, you will not have smooth sailing. Life will feel bumpier.

Be mindful of the need to cultivate a healthy relationship with yourself first. Once you give fully to yourself, you'll be more equipped to give to others.

"Smile. It just feels better."

Smiling is an automatic feel-better for me. As the old saying goes, "Turn that frown upside down." I have found this to be true internally as well. When I turn that frown upside down on the outside, I feel better on the inside. It really does make a difference not only in the way I feel but in my environment. It is contagious and absolutely makes a difference in my relationship with myself and with others.

Let's face it, we don't always feel like smiling. There are times when you may feel that a smile is just not in the forecast. That's okay too. Take that time to nurture yourself even more.

"Do not spend time fretting over others' approval or disapproval."

In the era of social media, we've become obsessed with appearances. We've become exposed to everyone's opinion. What do you do when you can't win everyone over?

Stop fretting.

Don't fret over whether others approve or disapprove of you. Know that you are perfect and beautiful just the way you are. Seeking the approval or validation of others can be a never-ending search. Who, other than you, can assess the value of the path you're on?

There is certainly nothing wrong with validation, and it feels good to be validated. But the issue comes in when you try to change who or what you are to fit in.

My mother used to say to me all the time, "people are going to always talk." Oh, how right she was.

Run your race. Follow your path. It will lead to a better relationship with self.

"Look at self in every situation."

It is easy to get caught up in the blame game. Blaming others for our situation or the way we feel has become a popular coping mechanism.

When confronted with a tough situation, I have found it both therapeutic and healing to look at self and ask, "What role did I play in this?"

Examining self is a perfect opportunity for growth. You are not blaming yourself. You are simply looking for areas of growth, so you don't repeat the pattern. Blaming others solves nothing. It only builds resentment and other negative emotions that end up being harmful to you and negatively affecting the relationship you have with yourself.

Every situation is a beautiful opportunity to grow in the relationship with yourself and refine who you want to be.

Look in the mirror, ask the hard questions, and move forward in a positive direction.

"Learn the lesson, forgive, and let go."

Forgiveness. It's a tough word to swallow.

There is so much to be said here, but it is straightforward. There is a lesson in everything. To have a good relationship with yourself, you must ask, "What is the lesson to be learned in this situation?" Then be willing to accept the lesson, forgive the situation, and let it go.

Forgiveness is essential to a healthy relationship with yourself.

"Stop trying to fit into the box that
someone else designed."

From the time we enter this world, we are told what to do and what not to do. We are also told what is right and what is wrong, as well as what to believe and what not to believe. It seems someone is always trying to make us into who and what they think we should be. In essence, it's like we are being put in a box.

It starts with our parents' saying things like "no," or affirming us as a "good boy" or "good girl" when we do exactly as they want. Then it progresses into the school where we are taught what to believe based on history and research. Then, of course, there is the church. In my experience the teachings of the church were fear-based. If you did not believe a certain way, you were destined for hell.

We carry this ideology into our adult lives even if it does not resonate with us. It is what we have been deeply indoctrinated to believe.

I am reminded of a story my mother told me. Every Easter she would cook a ham for Easter dinner. I noticed she would always chop off both ends of the ham before placing it in the pan. One year I asked her, "Why do you chop off the ends of the ham?" She replied, "It is what my momma always did.

So, I went to my grandmother and asked her, "Why do you chop off the ends of the ham?" She replied, "It is what my mother always did."

I then went to my great-grandmother and asked her, "Why do you chop off the ends of the ham?" She replied, "So it will fit in the pan that I have." At that point I just had to laugh. Even though my mother had a big enough pan, she still chopped off the ends of the ham because that is what she had always seen and been taught to do.

It is important to create the box that is *your* truth. Stand in your truth. No one's approval is needed for you to use the whole ham.

"Choose yourself."

To choose yourself first, you must feel worthy of that choice. I have struggled with this notion of worthiness much of my life. That feeling of unworthiness goes all the way back to my childhood. I have always been more concerned with others and making sure they were taken care of, often at the expense of myself. In the end, I neglected myself to please others.

There is certainly nothing wrong with caring but caring must start with self.

There is a reason that they always instruct you on the airplane to put the oxygen mask on yourself first before helping others.

Nurture yourself. Love yourself. Take care of yourself. Make yourself a priority. You deserve it.

"Show up for all aspects of your being and do it with care, acceptance, trust, and gentleness."

Make a commitment to start your day with some form of self-care. Accept yourself as you are regardless of the judgment and opinions of others. Trust your intuition and your inner guidance. Be gentle with yourself when you feel like you've failed. We all have.

All these things have certainly been a work in progress for me. Being gay in a society where it is unacceptable has made it challenging to accept myself. It has made it a challenge at times to be gentle with myself as opposed to judging and berating myself. When I started practicing self-care, I learned how to love myself better.

Regardless of your personal situation, practice care, acceptance, trust, and gentleness. Know that you are exactly where you need to be, doing exactly what you need to be doing at this very moment.

"Carve out time for fitness daily."

Take care of the temple you have been blessed with. Make time for fitness. As a nurse, I have witnessed thousands of people who failed to take care of their physical body. As a result, they were plagued with multiple health issues, and many transitioned too early in their life.

It all goes back to the relationship you have with yourself and the importance of nurturing that relationship first. Physical fitness is a very important aspect of that nurturing because it prioritizes self-care that further benefits your mind and spirit.

A lack of self-worth is often a barrier to taking the time to carve out fitness as a gesture of self-care. Show your body you love it!

You are worthy. Your physical, mental, and spiritual health depend heavily on a fitness routine.

Get started today.

"Let go of what is not for you, so you can make room for what is."

In my personal life, I have been guilty of holding on to what was not for me. Whether it be a job or relationship, I often held on out of fear and other negative emotions, at times not feeling like I deserved better.

I have always known in my spirit what was right, but I tended to argue with my spirit and tried to analyze the situation. *The spirit is always speaking, but many are seldom listening.* Listening to that gut feeling, inner guidance, or whatever you want to call it, will never lead you astray.

As I talked about earlier in the book, it is important to detach from the mental things holding you back and move into the heart space to get a clear answer about what to hold on to and what to let go of.

Remember, if it doesn't feel right, let it go and make room for what does feel right.

"Let the difficult, challenging times transform you, and they will."

We all go through difficult and challenging times in our lives. We have a choice during those times. We can accept and find the lesson, or we can fall into a pit of despair and dwell there feeling sorry for ourselves.

Everything unfolds as it is supposed to. This is a concept that can be hard to accept during rough times. The sudden tragic death of my mother was one of those times for me. It was difficult to accept and even more difficult to ask myself, "What is the lesson here?" It took me a long time, but that tragic situation transformed me in many ways.

We all have a story. The important part is to not let the story become our whole life. Don't carry the story around like a victim.

Be patient, trust the process, and allow the dark, tough times to create a better version of you.

"Remove the cloud that stands
between you and the sun."

Whatever your cloud may be, push it aside and allow the sun to penetrate your being.

Clouds have come in many different forms over the course of my life, such as family, friends, jobs, romantic relationships, and the list goes on. Clouds are nothing more than fog that has descended. The fog makes it more difficult to see. At times my biggest cloud is my mind. It has been all fogged up, completely blocking the sun and light from my vision.

Having an awareness of when relationships turn cloudy is an important step to moving toward where the sun is shining.

The sun is always shining somewhere, even when we can't see it. It will eventually make its way back around to us no matter how dark things feel. Seek out the sun.

"Failure is there to point you in a new direction."

Failure is part of life. It is how we learn best practice and eventually succeed. I have failed at relationships in my life, but they were great lessons that pointed me in a different direction. On several occasions, I had to fail at the same thing more than once before I learned the lesson. In other words, I failed the class and had to take it again.

It we never experience the wrong, we don't know what's right.

Be grateful for failure and keep trying until you get it right as opposed to beating yourself up over the failure. While it's something I have been guilty of over and over, eventually through failure I learned how to succeed in my own way.

We all fall. The question is, do we get up?

Get up and keep moving. Let the failure set you on a better path. A path of success.

"Leave behind that which no longer serves you."

I have found it important to be aware of my space. Am I in the right space? How am I feeling in this space?

Whether it be your job, your relationship, or your circle of friends, how are you feeling in that space? And how do you know if it's the wrong space?

It you are not feeling supported, encouraged, inspired, and uplifted in whatever space you are in, perhaps it is time to think about moving on.

For me, it is also about growth. Am I growing because of being in that relationship? Am I evolving and changing for the better? Am I learning new skills in the job? Does it give me fulfillment and satisfaction?

Ask these questions of yourself and take inventory of your spaces. Then leave behind that which no longer contributes to your life in a positive way.

"Step into your day with gratitude."

You cut yourself off from a supply of awesomeness when you are not in a state of gratitude. I read a quote somewhere that says, "The more you are grateful, the more the universe will give you to be grateful for."

On the contrary, the more you complain, the more the universe will give you to complain about. That's just the way universal law works.

It can be easy to complain but try starting your day with gratitude. It will create an improved relationship with self and those around you.

"Take time to simply *be*."

The simplest yet most complex verb of all: *to be.*

I am guilty of doing, doing, doing. Always trying to achieve. I often feel like I am more of a human *doing* as opposed to a human *being.* At times I even have difficulty sleeping at night because my brain will not shut off, constantly thinking of what I should be doing, could be doing, or want to be doing.

Part of nurturing the relationship with self is to take time to simply be. Do absolutely nothing but be.

Being give you time to rest, recuperate, reflect, and listen to your inner self. The noise that comes from always doing prevents rest, recuperation, reflection, and listening.

Take time to go sit somewhere comfortable and simply be. I enjoy sitting in nature or sometimes sitting in the middle of my bed looking out the window at the trees. Find a space that works for you. Find a time where you can embrace the quiet.

Take time to simply be with no agenda.

NURTURING NOTES

1. What is your perception of yourself? How do you see yourself?

   _____

   _____

2. What needs to change for you to improve the relationship with yourself?

   _____

   _____

3. How would you rate the relationship you have with yourself on a scale of 1-10 with 10 being great?

   _____

   _____

Phase Two:
Nurturing Notes for
a Better Relationship
with Your Mind

"Unplug from the source of all negative energy."

Everything is energy so is therefore transferrable. Energy—both positive and negative—is highly contagious. As the old saying goes: "It only takes one rotten apple to spoil the whole bunch." The same is true with energy. Just one person with negative energy can impact the whole environment.

Just like we unplug the lights at night so we can rest, we must also unplug the energy cord from other things to rest.

Unplug from negative energy so you can relax.

No one who sucks your energy, puts you down, makes you feel small, or is unloving towards you is entitled to your time—or your energy.

Whether it be family, friends, your work environment, your surroundings, or your mind, if it feels negative—UNPLUG!

Unplug the energy cord from that lamp and allow the mind to be peace.

"Moving forward often requires that we first go back."

I have found it difficult to truly live in the present without first dealing with the past. If I allowed the past to leave me with a troubled mind, eventually it forced me to deal with it so my mind can be at peace.

Most of us have things in our past that are not particularly pleasing, or things we may not be proud of. Things that trouble us if we allow them to. Dealing with those things, as opposed to pretending they don't exist, helps one to move on in a positive direction and cultivate a healthier relationship with the mind, soul, and body.

For me, dealing with a troubled childhood was the only way I could move forward as an adult. For many years I allowed childhood trauma to hold my mind hostage in a troubled state, and this influenced my relationship with self. Counseling and therapy took me back to my childhood and allowed me to deal with that trauma. I found freedom in facing that trauma once and for all.

Face the past. Deal with it in the best way that works for you. And finally, put it behind you.

"Create space between you and your thoughts."

The mind often works on autopilot with thousands of thoughts entering it every day, every hour, every minute. As my mom used to say, "You can't keep the birds from flying over your head, but you can keep them from building a nest in your hair." I love this saying because we can't necessarily keep the thoughts from coming, but we can decide which ones to give energy to through simply being aware.

I've learned to ask myself with every thought, *Is it true?* Our thoughts are very powerful tools, and they dictate our conditions and moods. Being aware of the thoughts, as opposed to just letting them run wild in your mind, affects your feelings and behaviors.

When you have a thought, pause, and create a little space. Space to think about that thought for a minute. Chances are the thought is basically bullshit and you can decide to delete it from your hard drive, which is your mind. Choose which thoughts to hold on to and which to let go of.

Deleting the lies leads to a healthier relationship with the mind.

"Healing begins on the inside before
it shows up on the outside."

Healing begins in the mind. Once again, it is about being aware of your thoughts.

As a Registered Nurse for the past thirty-three years, I have witnessed so much of what the mind can do to someone who has just received a diagnosis. The patients who decide to keep a positive mindset always have better outcomes. It all starts in the mind. The mind-body connection is real. Genuine. Powerful.

Our thoughts are manifested in our physical body, which makes it of utmost importance to let the healing begin in the mind.

For me, my troubled mind led to physical symptoms such as generalized discomfort, irregular bowel habits, and an overall sense of not feeling well. Once I decided to deal with what troubled me, I noticed a change in how I felt physically. The aches and pains went away. I had more energy. I felt better about myself. It is a process for me. If I allow myself to go back to being troubled in the mind, the physical symptoms reappear.

Stay aware of what is going on in your mind in an effort be whole. The care you give your mind will manifest in the care of your body.

"Do not allow external factors to block your vision. "

Situations and people can have a significant impact on our journey for the good or bad.

I remember when I decided to attend nursing school, the pastor and his wife at my church said, "That is not your calling." Your calling is to continue to play the piano in church." Then of course my mind kicked into high gear with all the doubt about whether I could complete nursing school.

I knew deep in my spirit that nursing was my vocational calling, but I allowed others and my mind to instill doubt and fear. Their words pushed me off course because I let them.

Follow your path, whether others understand it or not. Follow your path even when others disagree. It is *your* path. Do not allow anything, including your mind or any person, to block that path or that vision. If your spirit guides you, follow it!

"Bloom where you are."

There have been so many times where I've found myself in the desert. Dark and dry. A place where seemingly nothing would bloom. This sensation goes back to the mind and our relationship with the mind. We each have the capability to bloom where we are, even if it is in the desert. Be the light in that dark space.

Have you ever seen a flower grow up from the concrete? I have. It was an epiphany moment for me when I saw it. Beauty amid something so plain reminded me that we can bloom right where we are. We bloom because the light warms the surface and provides the nurturing environment in which the seed can flourish. The light nurtures what is beneath the surface—no matter how rough or dry or unpleasant the surface may seem.

We cannot allow circumstances to determine whether we blossom. Blossom despite the environment around you. Blossom right where you stand.

There is magic right where you are.

"Silence is where new ideas,
thoughts, and inspiration are born."

54 | Vince Shifflett

Life gets busy with so much external stimuli crowding the mind. As a writer, I have really learned the importance of silence. The quieter I become, the more I hear.

With the television, the smart phones, and tablets, the mind barely has time to embrace silence and rest. I have found that turning all devices off and sitting in complete stillness to be very therapeutic on many levels. It also increases my overall sense of well-being and decreases my stress levels.

Tune out and tune in to self to allow your mind to discover new ideas, thoughts, and inspiration.

I have found it helpful to schedule silent time on my calendar, just like I schedule every other appointment. It may be your most important appointment of the day.

"Life is what we make it from within and never without."

Everything begins and ends in the mind. Our mind affects our life. It affects how we see life. It affects how we live life. It affects the outcome of our life.

The mind is what we are using to change ourselves. Outside of meditation or very deep prayer, many of the self-growth techniques involve working with the mind. Healthy body is largely governed by being in right mind. Folks who are not in a great mind space often find it very difficult to care for the body. It gets down to the old adage, "Mind over matter."

Having a good relationship with your mind is essential to having a good life. That good relationship requires mindfulness. Being mindful of our thoughts. Being mindful of how we feel inside. Being mindful of what our inner guidance—our intuition—is telling us.

It all starts on the inside and manifests on the outside.

"See the good and beauty all around you."

You can focus on what is uncomfortable, challenging, and what you don't have... or you can focus on what is good and beautiful. It's your choice.

When I am feeling in a funk, I can simply sit on my back deck and look around. So much beauty. The trees and their many shades of color. The beautiful variety of birds singing in the chorus. The squirrels jumping from tree to tree and rustling in the leaves on the ground. The amazingly stunning and vast sky. I could go on and on. The point is, there is ALWAYS something incredible to focus on when the mind tries to see the negative.

Choose the delightful over the detrimental.

"Love no matter what. "

It is my belief that we are not in this world to tolerate each other, but instead we are here to love each other.

Don't allow situations or people to create a barrier between you and your ability to give love. Yes, it can be challenging when someone cuts you off in traffic or jumps in front of you at the grocery store line. It can be challenging when a co-worker attempts to push all your buttons. Or when someone gets argumentative with you on social media.

This is your perfect opportunity to love no matter what.

It will lead to peace in your mind. Love nurtures the mind. It is like food for the soul.

"Be the reason someone realizes
how simple it is to be nice. "

Don't affirm negative energy by reacting negatively. Be nice and transform it into positive energy.

I have come to realize that being nice is more for me than the other person. It just feels better to be nice. It's invigorating to offer a smile instead of a scowl. It is difficult at times? Absolutely. But it will be far healthier for the relationship you have with your mind. A relationship that is vital for all other relationships in your life.

"Stop trying to make sense of everything."

Everything will not always make sense. That is where *trust* comes in. Trust in something bigger than yourself. I love the scripture in the traditional Bible that says, "Lean not onto thy own understanding."

Trying to understand everything will lead to a troubled mind. In the case of the ending of my eighteen-year relationship, I drove myself crazy trying to understand and make sense of the whole situation. Why did it end? What did I do wrong? "It was supposed to last forever."

I continued with this rhetoric in my mind for over a year, causing myself much distress and sadness.

Through therapy and the support of many friends, I was finally able to simply accept it without trying to overanalyze and make sense of it all. Getting to a place of acceptance and trust allowed me to move on and maintain a more peaceful mindset.

Many things in your life may not make sense. Just trust that things happen exactly when and how they are supposed to. It is all part of life's lesson for our personal growth, and it will liberate you in an incredible way.

NURTURING NOTES

1. What are some ways you calm your mind?

   _____

   _____

2. What are some external distractions that you can eliminate for greater peace of mind?

   _____

   _____

3. How would you describe your current state of mind?

   _____

   _____

Phase Three: Nurturing Notes for Better Relationship with Spirit

"Spirit is always speaking but we are seldom listening."

Spirit, inner guidance, intuition or whatever you choose to call it, is always guiding us. Some call it that "gut feeling." The issue for me is feeling the need to argue with spirit or question spirit as opposed to simply listening and obeying.

I love the story of Jonah and the Whale in the traditional bible. Spirit was speaking to Jonah to go one way and he chose to go another way. As a result, he ended up in the belly of a whale. Doesn't sound like a place I want to be even though I have found myself there many times.

We can avoid a lot of heartache and disappointment simply by listening to spirit. Staying connected to spirit. It just always takes a mindful awareness. I think we all get disconnected at times. It is important to be aware when we do and get ourselves reconnected through whatever means works for us. That connection to spirit is a vital part of wholeness.

"Talk Less~Listen More."

The report my parents always received from my schoolteachers was, "he's a great student but he talks too much in class." It is impossible to talk and fully listen at the same time.

In our relationship with spirit, it is important to get quiet and listen. Too much chatter on our part blocks out what spirit is trying to say leading to a disconnection. That chatter can be internal chatter in the mind or external verbal chatter. The key is to get quiet.

Getting quiet has been a life changer for me. Learning to get quiet in the mind can be the most challenging part. I can be quiet and not talk out loud verbally but shutting up the mind is another story. Talking less is both about verbal talk and your mind talking.

Find a space where you can be alone and be quiet. Get quiet, get in the Zone, and get in touch with source energy. I do this through meditation which allows me to sync up with source.

I have grown to love the silence. It is when I am most inspired because I can hear. Hear my inner self.

"It is far more important to be the church as opposed to just attending church."

Given my upbringing, I simply could not talk about spirit without talking about the church.

Many equate the brick and mortar building we call the "church" to spirit. The two are not synonymous.

The brick-and-mortar building can be a place to connect with spirit if that works for you, but it alone is not spirit.

I have discovered that the church/sanctuary is inside of me, and I can tap into it when I need to. I am the church.

Growing up in church, I witnessed many who attended the church (the physical building), but their actions did not line up with spirit. We must be the church, not just go to church if we choose to even go at all.

We went to church 3-4 times a week in my home growing up. Going to church does not make you the church. My mother used to say, "living in a barn doesn't make you a horse any more than going to church makes you a Christian."

Taking a walk-in nature has turned out to be a great church/sanctuary for me. No distractions. The walk-in nature is a means of building a connection. A focus on the feeling – particularly the sensory aspect, including the esoteric aspects such as feeling "lighter" or "weight lifted off my shoulder" or feeling more "lighthearted" are ways of connecting deep within yourself. You don't need a building full of people to make a connection. Yet, if full of wonderful people, that too is making a connection. Tuning into those pleasant feelings is what you want. Knowing what is pleasant for you helps us feel whole. It's a knowing what your best self is that can help you stay connected with it.

Find your inner church/sanctuary and spend there on a regular basis.

"We Attract what we are."

This is a foundational spiritual law. We attract what we are.

Everything that goes out is coming back. So, then the question becomes, what are you putting out?

If you want love, send love out. This is great once your love is pure. It may be rather full of debris, which others can feel as heavy and needy.

If you want peace, be peaceful in all situations

If you want kindness, be kind to all

If you want happiness, put happiness out there for yourself and others.

Bottom line, put great things in the Universe and know that great things will return. Attracting what it is that you want and/or desire is all about you.

Make sure you are attracting what you desire by staying connected to spirit. Spirit will never lead you astray. That connection can help you clean up your love. The challenge for most people is they don't know how to make their own connection. Most need to have a person to connect with. The concept of connecting with spirit is too abstract. Telling folks how to connect is very helpful for many.

"There's a purpose in your path. Stay the Course."

Sometimes the path may get rough and rocky. Sometimes we stumble upon a block in the way. Do we turn around or do we push forward and stay the course?

Life is full of challenges on our path. The key to success is staying the course. Not stopping or turning around when we run into a roadblock.

Be patient and take that time to connect to spirit and let it guide you. In order to do this, you have to let go. Letting go is the challenge. Many don't know what that means.

There are really no obstacles, just ways around them. Stay the course on your path.

Others may not understand your path or agree with your path. They don't need to. Again, it is your path. Stay connected to spirit as your guide and keep marching forward.

"Sometimes self-discovery requires self-destruction."

There are times when we must destroy old thoughts, old beliefs, and old ways of doing things. We must self-destruct those old things for the emergence of the new. To discover the new, the old must die.

Hanging on to the past is a barrier to moving forward on the path that spirit is guiding us on.

When we self-destruct, we are free to truly discover the underlying self. The true self as opposed to the self that our mind and our past tells us that we are.

We are spirit living in a human body and sometimes our humanness just gets in the way. That is when the destruction must begin.

In the city I live in, they are tearing down old run-down buildings and building beautiful new development.

Tear down that which does not serve your better good and make room for new development.

The destruction phase can be painful but what emerges from the rubble will be amazingly beautiful.

"Being spiritual does not require attending a church, synagogue, mosque, or other physical structure."

Spirituality is a broad concept with room for many interpretations. For me, it feels like a sense of connection to something bigger than myself and seeking a meaningful connection with that something bigger. So how do you get there? Do you let go? How did you know you were not your "best self" without a connection to spirit? When did you realize you don't need another person or other people to feel whole? The wholeness is being secure in yourself. The people are the icing on the cake.

Church can be a part of your spiritual practice, but it is certainly not required.

I have found many religious people who attend church to be extremely judgmental, righteous, and outright mean at times. For example, I was ousted from my position as the piano player in a very large Christian church when they found out I was gay. It seems they loved me until they found out. They were less than loving about their decision. Being spiritually connected requires three virtues which include compassion, empathy, and open heartedness. I felt none of the three from the deacon board that ousted me.

In my experience, church was more about religion and less about spirituality and our connection to our spiritual being. Religion is about right and wrong whereas spirituality is about purpose and love. Sadly, I found the church to be far more religious than spiritual.

If you want to be a spiritual person, let kindness be your guiding light. Kindness towards self-first, then kindness towards others and towards the planet as well as all of creation. This will surely lead you down a path towards a deeper connection with your spiritual self. Simply being a more loving human being in thought, word, and deed. We all must know our best self. The process of getting to know our best self is where kindness comes in. Kindness is only one tool. If kindness means sitting and doing nothing to work on yourself, that's not kindness. It's laziness. I have seen that a lot with people.

"Let yourself be surprised at how prevalent beauty is when you simply stop, look, and listen."

Stop: Pause and notice your breath. Be grateful for your breath as it enters and exits your body. Gratitude is a great way to stay connected to spirit

Look: Look at all the beauty around you

Listen: Listen to spirit~Let it be your guide.

Stopping, looking, and listening are all part of being aware. We know by now that it takes awareness to be connected to spirit.

Step out of your routine and take time to just stop, look around, and listen.

You'll be amazed at what you see and hear.

"Understanding one's many inner lives are
essential to connecting with spirit."

I keep seeing on the news where we are very focused on exploring outer space. Spending lots of money and time to visit other planets.

It seems that western culture is structed in such a way that silence and stillness are the exception and not the rule. Both are essential components to connecting with spirit.

Take more time to explore your inner space as opposed to your outer space. Many don't know how to do this. Resourcing, as I mentioned earlier, is a place to begin. Grounding is also a place to begin. Understanding one's inner space is vital to acting more wisely in the world. That inner space is where the spiritual connection takes place.

"Become vital, awake, and aware in all areas of your life."

Becoming implies it is a journey and not a destination. I don't think anyone is connected to spirit 100% of the time. We all experience periods of disconnection. Spirituality is a vital awareness that pervades all realms of our being. It is a way of being in the world.

How are you being? Are you being compassionate? Are you being loving? Are you being kind? That is spirituality. It is the very core of our being. It is being vital, awake, and aware in all areas of our life.

I work on staying connected to my spiritual being by expanding my awareness, transforming my inner demons, trying to make conscious choices, and clarifying my purpose. Again, this is not a one and done. It is a consistent practice.

It is easy to go through life on autopilot completely unaware. Have you ever driven home from somewhere and not remember the drive home because your mind was elsewhere? I have. Being connected to spirit is being in the moment. When the mind starts to stray, and it will, be aware of that and bring it back to the here and now. Bring it back and plug in to your connection.

"Being disconnected from spirit
will leave you in the dark."

I've lost count of how many times I've found myself disconnected from spirit. Lost. Void. Stumbling around not knowing which way to go.

Even though I talk about it, write about it, speak on it at conferences, and even counsel people about it, I still find myself disconnected at times in complete utter darkness.

It's kind of like going to nail salon for a manicure and noticing the manicurist nails are dirty and unkept. They can get your nails looking beautiful, but their nails are a hot mess. I feel the same at times when it comes to what I talk and write about. I can talk and write about it but still struggle with it myself.

Knowing your best self is what this is about. You must sense/feel what it is to know when you are not there. At that point, you must have tools to get back to your best self. Resourcing. Grounding.

It's just a gentle reminder of the importance of staying connected to let the light guide us. To prevent us from spending too much time in the dark.

NURTURING NOTES

1. What is your definition of Spirit?

    _____

    _____

2. What are some ways that you stay connected to spirit?

    _____

    _____

3. Do you feel connected or disconnected right now?

    _____

    _____

4. How do you feel when you are connected versus disconnected?

    _____

    _____

Phase Four:
Nurturing Notes for
Better Relationship
with Your
Significant Other

"Love cannot flourish on autopilot."

Love takes attention, recommitment, and rededication. It takes nurturing. Nurturing requires our time, which can often get put on the backburner when we're busy or distracted by life's demands. But if you neglect your relationships, they'll suffer for it.

I am guilty of taking my relationship for granted. Of simply assuming my partner would always be there. I love the old saying, "Whatever you did to get them, you must continue to do in order to keep them."

I think this is true. We get too comfortable and forget to nurture the relationship. If we want it to continue and grow, we must give it our attention. We must make that connection. Recommit to that person. Repeatedly. It must be a conscious effort.

Nothing truly flourishes on autopilot. Even the plants in your home need attention and care. The same is true for your relationship with the ones you love.

"How are you showing up in your
relationship with your partner?"

Are you showing up as your true authentic self from the start, or are you showing up like what you think your partner wants?

The biggest lesson I took away from an eighteen-year relationship was to always be myself as opposed to trying to be what he wanted me to be. Be real from the start. Be authentic. Be *you*.

We have all heard the saying, "Put your best foot forward." My question is, what about that other foot? That foot with the big corn on your toe. Your partner will eventually see it, so I think it is best to put both feet forward in the beginning.

Step into your relationship with awareness. Awareness of your relationship history. What kind of relationships do you aspire to have? Some may need a strong friendship, others need passionate romance, others thrive on sex, and some need it all. There's no wrong answer to what you need out of a relationship, but there is a wrong partner who may not naturally fill that need. If you are aware of your needs, you'll be more likely to choose a relationship that complements you both. Though keep in mind that it even the *right* person may not be able to sustain the "all" over time, which is why nurturing the relationship can help fuel one another.

Entering a relationship with expectations of what it "should be" inhibits our ability to understand our role in the relationship. Instead of expectations, ask questions. Be curious. Enter with self-awareness. Self-awareness helps identify our strengths and weaknesses when we come into a new relationship. Be open to what "could be" as opposed to the expectation of what "should be."

As you bring your authentic self into the relationship and look at what it "could be" with the right care, you'll grow both as a person and a partner.

"Be a partner, not a parent."

There is a fine line between being a partner versus being a parent. I am guilty in previous relationships of moving into a parental role. Asking questions like, "Where have you been?" "I tried to call, but you didn't answer your phone." "Why are you so late coming home from work today?" "Who was that on the phone?" Those are all questions a parent would ask a child.

It all comes down to trust, and that trust must start with self.

Love your partner and allow them to be. Allow them to go, do, be, and enjoy life. If there is mutual trust, love, and respect, it's safe to let each of you grow individually and have parts of your life that may not be tied to your partner. Of course, I am not endorsing infidelity done in secret to meet the needs in a relationship that your partner can't meet. But I am endorsing honesty, conversation, and individual growth so that you can fulfill all areas of your life.

Encourage partnering in your relationship, not parenting.

"There's a fine line between dependence and independence."

think it is natural and even beautiful to be dependent on your partner—to a certain degree. On the other hand, it is equally as important to be independent. You had a life before you met your partner, and they had a life before they met you. Maintaining parts of that life is essential.

Maintaining the friendships and continuing to enjoy what you like is vital. What you enjoy may not be what your partner enjoys, and that is fine. That is healthy.

I made the mistake in previous relationships of sticking together like peanut butter and jelly. Where you saw one, you saw the other. There seems to be a tendency to greatly decrease or even cut off communication with our friends or family once we find that special One. A tendency to start doing everything *they* want to do and forgetting the things *you* love to do.

It is important to remain free without becoming what your partner or spouse wants you to be.

Dependence and independence are both okay when balanced properly.

"The best way to love your partner or spouse is not to try to change them".

True love is about accepting others just the way they are. If there are behaviors or things that they are doing that you feel you cannot tolerate, have a conversation. If it's a deal-breaker, it may mean that you must move on, but that is a better option than trying to change them.

Now that you have them, you decide you don't like the way they dress. So, you take them shopping and convince them to buy clothes and dress the way you like. True story. Does their style look old-fashioned to you? Are you embarrassed to be seen with your partner because of the way they dress? Does it take the romance down a notch? It is important to investigate what is bothering you about them. Did you know that Prince Phillip never liked Queen Elizabeth's hair because it was too old-fashioned? In the scheme of things, is what you want to change important enough to leave the relationship over? If not, then perhaps your demands are what need to be changed, not the person.

Allow them to be exactly who and what they want to be.

"Beautiful things happen in our relationship when we start to *see* each other."

W e can be looking and not see. We can be listening and not hear.

It is important to see your partner and let them know that you see them. Kind gestures and comments are a great way to do this.

If you know your partner values physical appearance, you can *see* them through how you uplift them: "You look beautiful in that outfit." "I noticed your new hairstyle and I love it." "That color looks awesome on you." Keep in mind that compliments can be very uplifting if sincere, and even if not, if it's not manipulative, they are a great asset in a relationship.

If your partner values their creative art, notice and praise their work. Once you know your partner and what's important to them, you can *see* and *hear* them through it and connect with it by encouraging them.

Let your partner know you see them. Look into their eyes. Once again, *seeing* one another is about connection. Looking in their eyes is an intimate reflection of what's going on in the relationship or in the other person's day. As they say, "The eyes are the window to the soul."

The beauty of your relationship will grow as you intentionally make that connection.

"Love is a verb."

Showing your partner love through your actions is essential, as opposed to just saying, "I love you."

Words are extremely powerful. They can build up or tear down a relationship. Words are important but they DO need to be backed up by action. For me it is more about the sincerity of the words and not just the words themselves.

What are you doing (action) to show your partner how much they mean to you? It can be something as simple as a text message in the morning that says, "Have a great day, love." Or it can be a random surprise like bringing home flowers for your partner.

Whatever you choose, make sure you are *showing* love and not just *saying* love. What you choose should be based on your partner's love language. Knowing the other person's love language—whether it is time together, acts of kindness, words of affirmation, gifts, or whatever is meaningful to them—is vital to knowing what expresses love to them. In other words, we all express love in a different way. Show that love through action.

"Let go of the idea that you alone are responsible for every single one of your partner's needs."

It has always been my personal belief that you cannot get everything you need from one person. We get different things from different people. I get things from my friends that I do not get from my partner. It's a different kind of love.

I get things from my co-workers that I do not get from my partner. I learn and grow in a different way by spending time with different people. That need to learn and grow must come from multiple sources. Not just from you partner.

Consider which needs aren't getting met *by* you and *for* you. Being honest about that is key. As your relationship matures, you'll learn what roles you and your partner fulfill for each other, and what roles your outside friendships fulfill.

"There's no way to benefit your partner
unless you start with yourself."

When you create the perfect partner inside of yourself, the Universe will match it. Start with self. Start by creating in you what you desire in another.

Creating that perfect partner in yourself can be done in many ways. If you want a loving, compassionate companion, be loving and compassionate towards yourself. To break it down easily, whatever you desire in a partner, be that for yourself. In other words, you can be your best partner until he or she shows up in your life. And be okay with that. You cannot always control when or if you'll find the right partner, but you can control your happiness with yourself.

Healthy relationship with self is the key to healthy relationships with others.

Knowing your own path, finding someone who respects that path, and the ability to respect the other person in the same way is vital for a romantic relationship. Communication is key and knowing who you are is key. Don't be someone you are not.

NURTURING NOTES

1. How would you describe your relationship with your significant other? Healthy, Unhealthy, Needs work.............?

    _____

    _____

2. What can you personally do to improve the relationship you have with your significant other?

    _____

    _____

3. Are you allowing them to fully be themselves?

    _____

    _____

4. Are you acting like a partner or more like a parent?

    _____

    _____

5. Is your relationship adding to your personal growth and happiness?

    _____

    _____

6. Do you feel supported in your relationship?

_____

_____

CONCLUSION

Every single relationship benefits the evolution of our consciousness. They all have a purpose. Sometimes they hurt. Sometimes they bring us joy. None the less, they are sent our way as part of our purposeful path.

Peace, love, harmony, and stability in our relationships come from showing up every single day with a fresh desire for growth, intimacy, and goodness. This is true in all our relationships, including the relationship we have with ourselves. Relationships are an essential part of our life. They help us grow. They help us learn more about ourselves. They give us love and support. And they help us learn how to love and support others.

It is my relationships that have taught me the most about myself. The good, the bad, and the ugly. All a learning experience. Find the gratitude in all your relationships. Even the not-so-good ones.

It is my deepest desire that this book has given you reason to pause and think about your relationships, and to pursue and nurture beautiful, fruitful relationships moving forward in every area of your life.

Thank you so much for taking time to read my work. I am deeply grateful and look forward to hearing your thoughts!